LEGENDS
OF THE

Iroquois

LEGENDS
OF THE
Iroquois

As Told by
Tehanetorens
(Ray Fadden)

Book Publishing Company
Summertown, Tennessee

Copyright 1998 by Tehanetorens (Ray Fadden)

Cover painting by Kahionhes (John Fadden)
Cover design by Warren C. Jefferson and Jeffrey Clark

Illustrations: Kahionhes
Pictographs: Tehanetorens

Book Publishing Company
P.O. Box 99
Summertown, TN 38483

01 00 99 98   4 3 2 1

ISBN 1-57067-056-0

Tehanetorens
    Legends of the Iroquois / as told by Tehanetorens.
            p.   cm.
    ISBN 1-57067-056-0 : $9.95
    1. Iroquois Indians—Folklore. 2. Legends.—New York (State)
    I. Title
    E99.I7T45 1998

                                98-33967
                                CIP

This work is dedicated to my grandsons Donald, David, and Daniel, plus my great-grandsons Ian and Evan. This work is also dedicated to Apeta (Julian Harris), Miss Susan Kirkby, Mr. Hale Sipe, Tchanku Tanka (A. Hyatt Verrill), Tom Porter, Dick Laughing, Rita & Clarence White, George Buck, Alex Gray, Oren Lyons, Emily General, John Mohawk, Joann Reyome, Ernie Benedict, Mr. N. Miles, Mr. Orange O'Dell, A. W. Abbey, Mr. Carroll Fadden, Sr. and the young warriors of Akwesasne.

Legends of the Iroquois

Foreword

The Great Peace

Sometime in the centuries prior to the arrival of Europeans in North America, the Mohawk, Cayuga, Onondaga, Oneida, and Seneca Nations formed an alliance to establish the Great Peace, *Kaianerekowa*. Named the Iroquois Confederacy by the French and the League of the Five Nations by the English, the people called themselves the Haudenosaunee, the People of the Longhouse. Their primary geographic region was present-day New York State, but prior to the arrival of Europeans the Haudenosaunee dominated the land area extending from southeastern Quebec, west to the Ohio, and south to Georgia.

For many years the Haudenosaunee had been warring among themselves and with other nations, The stories tell of troubled times, of loss of life, even of cannibalism. Then a child was born whose lifework would be the founding of the Iroquois Confederacy. When Dekanawidah, the Peacemaker, and his helper, Hiawatha, traveled amongst the Haudenosaunee nations to convince them to join the Great Peace, the Haudenosaunee lived in rectangular houses called longhouses. Longhouses were constructed of bark, often elm, fastened over a cedar frame. They could be up to 200 feet long and had a door at each end. Sleeping accommodations and storage were arranged along the sides of the longhouse, and families would share the cooking and heating fires arranged down the center aisle. The family unit of the Iroquois was the clan, and each clan had its own villages.

Because all members of an Iroquois clan believed themselves to be descended from the same woman, all the people of the same clan living in a clan village were related. Women of the clan owned the houses and the fields. A woman's husband came from a different clan and moved to the village of his wife. Children were members of their mother's clan. If a husband and wife divorced, the man was expected to leave the village and return to his clan, taking only his personal possessions. An Iroquoian nation was comprised of the clans within the nation. For example, the Turtle clan, Wolf clan, and Bear clan were the original clans which comprised the Mohawk nation. All the clans could be signified by pictographs (see page 25).

Pictographs such as those presented in *Legends of the Iroquois* are the original writing system used by many Native American and First Nations (Canadian designation) peoples. Pictographs can be symbols of physical objects or of concepts. When the Iroquois Confederacy was established the visual symbols of the Confederacy were designated by the Peacemaker.

The Haudenosaunee League, said Dekanawidah, would be represented by a Longhouse. The easternmost of the Five Nations, the Mohawk Nation, was designated the keeper of the eastern door. The central fire of the Confederacy, the center of the Longhouse, would be the Onondaga Nation. As the westernmost nation, the Seneca Nation would be the keeper of the western door. Longhouse familial ties then extended from individual women and their families to the clan, from the clan to the nation, and from the nation to the Haudenosaunee, or Iroquois Confederacy. Because the intent was to establish peace among nations, the Confederacy intended to offer membership, called "extending the rafters" of the Longhouse," to other nations willing to live in accordance with Confederacy codes of conduct. Once the Tuscarora Nation accepted the invitation to join the Haudenosaunee in 1715, the Five Nations became the Six Nations.

For untold generations the people lived in accordance with the Great Law as it had been given to them by the Peacemaker. The story of the Founding of the League became the foundation of Haudenosaunee culture, explaining the sacred origin of certain religious beliefs, political organization, and social organization. Other stories told, for example, of the origin of the constellations, the discovery of fire, how birds got their songs, and how humans are to live with one another and the rest of creation. The Haudenosaunee prospered until there came from the east a new people, people very different from any they had known before.

Nadine N. Jennings

A Key to Six Nations Pictographs

Picture writing is a means of expressing thoughts or recording events by marks or drawings. An understanding of Iroquois or Six Nations customs, dress, history, culture, language, and tradition is necessary for the understanding of these pictograph signs. The symbols and signs given in this pamphlet, in most cases, originated in both ancient and modern Six Nations culture. Some of the more ancient signs were found on wampum belts, bark dishes, condolence canes, rock writing, bead work, and designs recorded in the writings of early missionaries and explorers who traveled among the Iroquois. In some cases, where a thought design was lacking, a general Indian design taken from the most important known pictographs of the North American Indians has been used. The designs collected and illustrated in this pamphlet have required a great deal of effort, thought, and research, because sources of information about them are very scarce.

From legends and traditions handed down to young Iroquois today, it is known that the old ones among the Iroquois had an elaborate system of pictograph writing. Each bark cabin had its clan symbol painted over the entrance. Records of the happenings and exploits of the Iroquois were painted inside the bark houses. Bark was stripped from a tree exposing the whitened wood. This made an excellent surface for presenting pictographs. In some cases a post was erected in the village to display pictographs. In every town of the Six Nations the War Chief erected a war-post upon which great events were recorded. Many of these memorial posts have been mentioned in the writings of early explorers. In the *Moravian Journals* and the *Jesuit Relations* picture writings of the Iroquois are often mentioned. The following quotations are examples of this:

> Their ancestors were well aware, that they were in need of something to enable them to convey their ideas to a distant nation, or preserve the memory of remarkable events. To this end they invented something like hieroglyphics, and also strings and belts of Wampum. Their hieroglyphics are characteristic figures, which are more frequently painted upon trees than cut in stone. They are intended either to caution against danger, to mark a place of safety, to direct the wanderer into the right path, to record a remarkable transaction, or to commemorate the deeds and achievements of their celebrated heroes, and are as intelligible to them, as a written account is to us.

> The warriors sometime paint their own deeds and adventures. Other paintings point out the places where a company of Indians have been hunting, showing the nights they spent there, the number of deer, bear, etc., killed during the hunt, etc. If even a party of traveling Indians have spent but one night in the woods, it may be easily known,

not only by the structure of their sleeping huts, but by their marks on the trees, to what tribe they belonged; for they always leave a mark." (*History of the Mission of The United Brethren Among The Indians in North America*, by George Henry Leskiel.)

C. Colden, writing of the war parties of the Iroquois, says that after traveling about three or four miles from their village:

They always peel a large piece of bark from some great tree; they commonly chose an oak, as more lasting; upon the smooth side of this wood they, with their red paint, draw one or more canoes, going from home, with the number of men in them paddling, which go upon the expedition, and some animal, as a deer or fox. An emblem of the nation against which the expedition is designed, is painted at the head of the canoes; for they always travel in canoes along the rivers, which lead to the country against which the expedition is designed, as far as they can. After the expedition is over, they stop at the same place on their return. They represent on the same or some tree near it the event of their enterprise, and now the canoes are painted with their heads toward the town; the number of the enemy killed is represented by scalps painted black, and the number of prisoners by as many withes (sticks for binding), and (with) which they usually pinion their captives. These trees are the annals, or rather trophies, of the Five Nations. I have seen many of them, and by them and their war songs, they preserve the history of their great achievements. (*The History of the Five Nations*, by Hon. Cadwallader Colden, p. XXV-XXVI.)

Adadarhoh		Barrel (fire water)	
Adadarhoh		Bear	
		Bear	
Akwesasne		Bear tracks	
Arrow Algonquin		Beaver	
Arrow Iroquois		Beaver	
Arrow			
Ask aid of the Creator		Beaver in lodge	
Basket		Beaver in lodge	
		Black robe Priest	
Bark barrel		Bone fishhooks	
		Boy	
Bark rattle			
Bark tray		Broom	

Buffalo	Canoe on river
Bug	Canoe on lake
Burden strap	Canoe — seven warriors
Bowl	White man in canoe
Bark sled	Celestial trees
Blow gun and darts	Celestial tree resting on sky dome
Cabin	
Eagle Dance Wing	Covenant chain, symbol of peace
Camp fire	Chain of alliance
Canada, Christian	Chiefs
Canoe	
Canoe	Chief calling people to council
Canoe, Dugout	

Clan mother nominating Chief	
Cloud	
Cloud, rain	
Cloud, snow	
Cooking	
Cooking	
Come	
Corn	
Corn pounder	
Council fire	

Cradle board	
Heron / Crane	
Crooked tongue, liar / Forked tongue, liar	
Crow	
Sun (day)	
Dead	
Dead	
Dead fall	
Death / Sleep	
Deer	
Doe / Dead deer	
Antler war club	

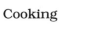

Dew eagle

Direction

Dishonesty, crooked trail

Dog

Dream

Drink

Drowning

Drum

Ducks

Eat

Eel

Turtle Clan   Eel Clan
(in council)

Elk

Error in song

Evening, Sunset

Eagle

Eagle feathers

Earthen vessel, Iroquois

Vessel, Algonquin

Face, stone giant

Face, hurricane

Fire

Fire water

Fish

Five Nations
  war against
  common enemy

Five United
  Iroquois Nations

Flowers

Flute

Fox

Friends,
  allies

Friendship

Friendship

Frog

Gave
  skins
  and meat

Gave skins

Geese

Gourd rattle

Grass

Sky dome, Tree
  of Life,
  Sun

Great Spirit
  speaks

Happiness
  in heart,
  Sun heart

Hawk,
  swiftness

Many

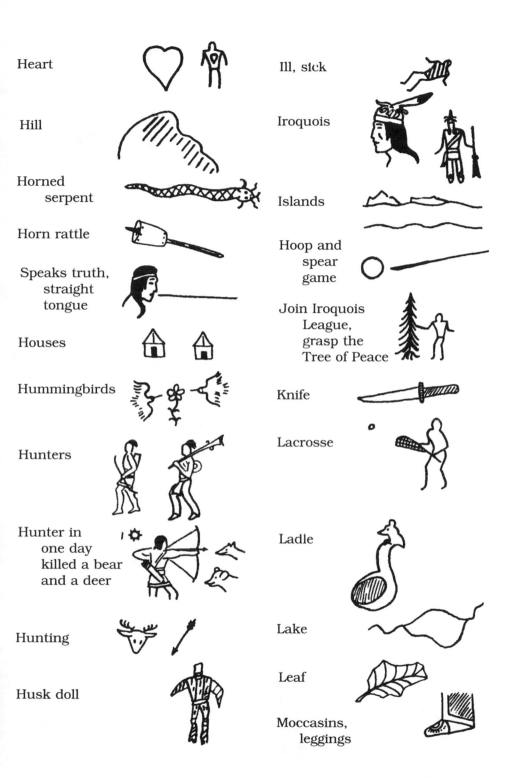

Heart

Hill

Horned
   serpent

Horn rattle

Speaks truth,
   straight
   tongue

Houses

Hummingbirds

Hunters

Hunter in
   one day
   killed a bear
   and a deer

Hunting

Husk doll

Ill, sick

Iroquois

Islands

Hoop and
   spear
   game

Join Iroquois
   League,
   grasp the
   Tree of Peace

Knife

Lacrosse

Ladle

Lake

Leaf

Moccasins,
   leggings

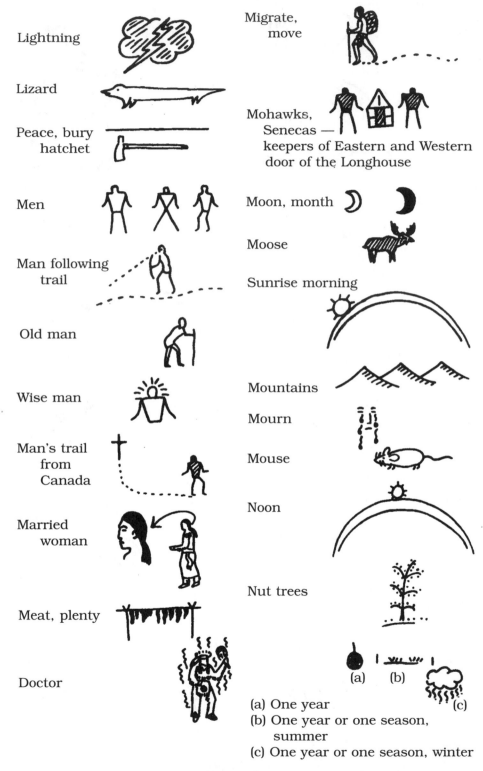

Lightning

Lizard

Peace, bury hatchet

Men

Man following trail

Old man

Wise man

Man's trail from Canada

Married woman

Meat, plenty

Doctor

Migrate, move

Mohawks, Senecas — keepers of Eastern and Western door of the Longhouse

Moon, month

Moose

Sunrise morning

Mountains

Mourn

Mouse

Noon

Nut trees

(a)   (b)   (c)

(a) One year
(b) One year or one season, summer
(c) One year or one season, winter

18

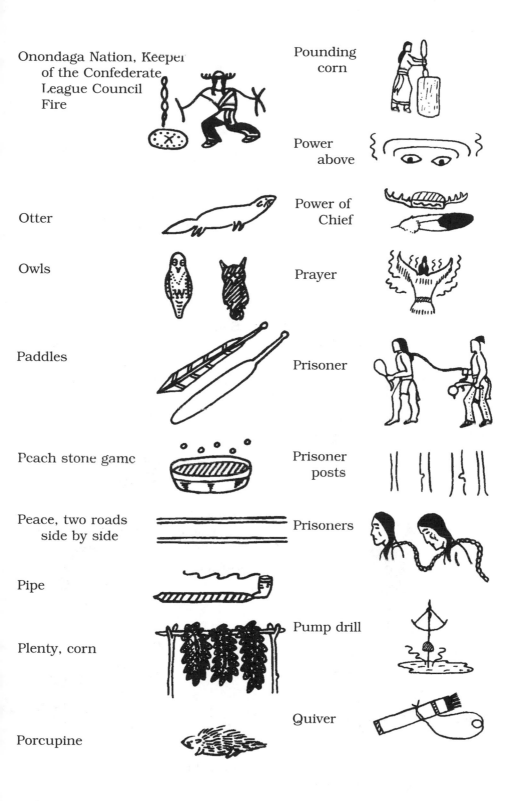

Onondaga Nation, Keeper of the Confederate League Council Fire

Otter

Owls

Paddles

Peach stone game

Peace, two roads side by side

Pipe

Plenty, corn

Porcupine

Pounding corn

Power above

Power of Chief

Prayer

Prisoner

Prisoner posts

Prisoners

Pump drill

Quiver

Rabbit

Rattlesnake

Rat

River

Road

Sadness, black heart

Sacred (Sun) Woman

Sea

See

Seek new hunting grounds

Skinny

Shoot

Shoot arrow

Shoot gun

Sing with drum

Snake

Snare

Snowshoe

Snow snake

Speak

(a)

(b)

(a) & (b) Speaks at Council

Speak together	
Spirits	
Squash rattle	
Squirrel	
Stars	
Starvation	
Stone axe	
Sturgeon	
Sun	
Sunset	
Sunrise	
Sun, stars, moon	

Celestial Tree, Sun	
Thunder Spirit	
Tobacco plant	
Tomahawk	
To take shelter beneath the Tree of Peace (Iroquois Confederacy)	
Trader, White man	
Trail	
Trail	
Trail crossed river	
Trees	
Tree	

21

Tree of Peace

or Iroquois Government resting on the world

Tree of upper world

Turkey

Turtle

Turtles

Turtle shell rattle

Two suns, two days

Two nations unite

tadpole

Unity of the Five Nations

Villages

Unmarried woman

Wampum belts and strings

War

War

War belt

War club

Warrior

War post

Water

Warrior bearing scalps

Water drum

Water falls

Women

Woman, dead

Wolf

World

Wounded by arrow

Wounded six times

Longhouse

Gave belts to raise war party

Mud hen

Gull

Partridge

Spring, small grass

Summer, tall grass

Fall, little snow

Winter, deep snow

Mountain lion

Symbols of the Six Nations (Iroquois Confederacy)

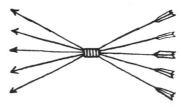

Five united brothers, the Five Nations plus the sixth brother, Tuscarora, after 1712.

Tree of Peace, a white pine with the weapons of war buried beneath.

Belt of Five Nations, the white heart or tree in the center is Onondaga, capital of the Confederacy.

Five bound arrows, for the Five Nations

Longhouse with six fires for the Six Nations.

Circle with mark in center symbolizes the Five Nations.

The record of an Iroquois Warrior as displayed in his cabin.
- (a) The number of times he has been wounded
- (b) He has twice been to war without returning
- (c) He was wounded by an arrow
- (d) He gave belts to raise a war party
- (e) He has gone back to fight before returning home
- (f) He killed a man who had a bow and arrow
- (g) (h) He took two men and a woman prisoner

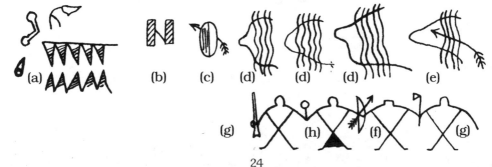

The Clans of the Six Nations

Below are the clans of the Iroquois. Every warrior and woman of the Iroquois belonged to one of these clans. Clan members considered each other as brothers and sisters. No one could marry into his or her own clan. The children belonged to the clan of their mother. Clan members of one tribe were given welcome, food, and shelter by clan members of another tribe. The clan system united the Iroquois into a strong brotherhood.

Bear Clan   Deer Clan   Snipe Clan   Beaver Clan

Turtle Clan

Wolf Clan   Heron Clan   Eel Clan   Eagle Clan

Mohawk,   Onondaga,   Seneca,
People of Flint   Hill People   People of Great Mountain

Oneida,   Cayuga, People of the   Tuscarora,
People of   Great Pipe or Swamp   People of the Shirt
Standing Stone   People

An Akwesasne Hike

An Akwesasne hike as illustrated by Joan White, aged 12, member of grade seven of the Mohawk Indian School, Hogansburg, New York.

It was on the twenty-fourth day of Sept. (twenty four Suns of the harvest moon)

They climbed Mohawk Mountain and ate their lunch there.

A group of Mohawks left Akwesasne (the Place Where the Partridge Drums)

After that nineteen climbed Indian Mountain

They left early in the morning

There were four adults or chiefs (teachers)

and sixteen went back to the truck.

There were twenty three boys

and twelve girls.

Afterward they met at Latonka Cabin. They ate a lunch there.

They all got into a truck.

They headed south.

Toward evening they left the mountain country, and,

They headed for the Adirondack Mountains. On the way they saw many mountains, rivers and trees.

getting into the truck, they headed for Akwesasne, the Place Where the Partridge Drums.

On the way back to Akwesasne the truck lights went out. It was very dark.

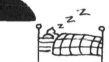

They had to follow a car in order to see the road.

After a while they arrived at Akwesasne, Mohawk Country.

That night they slept heavily and they were very tired.

The End

Great Bear
(North Wind)

Great Panther
(West Wind)

Great Moose
(East Wind)

January,
Snow Moon

March,
Wind Moon

April,
Maple Sugar Moon

May,
Planting Moon

June,
Strawberry Moon

July,
Thunder Moon

August,
Green Corn Moon

September,
Harvest Moon

October, Leaf
Falling Moon

November, Hunting
Moon

December,
Long Night Moon

Beaver tail symbolizes
peace and plenty

Little Fawn
(South Wind)

Conservation
As the Indian Saw It

Many moons ago (arrow going back)

Before the white man came

the Indian had sunshine in his heart.

There were many great forests in America.

There were many animals in America.

There were many birds in America.

There were many fish in the rivers.

There were many fur-bearing animals.

The Indian had lived here in America for many, many years.

Then from the direction of the rising sun, across the waters, came a great winged canoe.

In it was the white man.

With his axe he cut down too many trees.

With his thunder gun he exterminated the animals, the deer, bear, and other forest creatures.

He, the white man, took too many fish from the streams.

He, the white man, destroyed too many birds. He plowed up too much land.

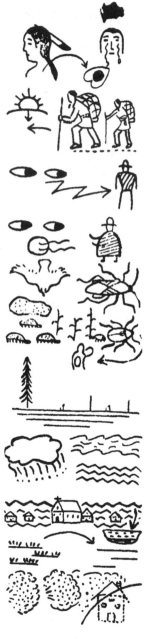

It was not good and the Indian became sad.

He had pain in his heart.

He moved westward toward the setting sun.

The Great Spirit was angry at the workings of the white man.

The Great Spirit said, "We will see the results of greed and waste."

Because there were no birds to eat the insects, the insects increased.

They ate the crops of the farmers.

Because there were no forests to hold back the soil,

The rains made many floods.

The rushing waters washed away the towns and farms of the white man. The waters ran wild carrying the soil to the sea.

Because there was no heavy sod, it having been destroyed by the white man, the winds tore up the soil and caused dust storms.

Dust and sand covered the farms of the white man.

The white man was sad. His heart dragged on the ground.

He said, "I have been a fool."

He said, "I must teach my children to be wiser than I have been."

He said, "I will tell them to plant trees on the earth.

Their roots will hold back the water and the earth."

He said, "I will put fish in the rivers.

They will eat the young of the mosquito and other harmful insects."

He said, "I will put houses in trees for the birds. The birds will eat the harmful insects."

He said, "If I do these things, God will smile on me again.

He will make this country as good and beautiful as it was before the white man, my ancestor, came here and destroyed it."

Gift of the
Great Spirit

The old Iroquois told this story to the young people to teach them to be kind to the aged.

Many winters and summers

in the past (arrow going back)

there was an Iroquois village.

One day an old man appeared at the edge of this village. The old man wore ragged clothes. He seemed very tired and looked hungry.

As he walked through the village, he looked over the door of each house. Over the doors of the bark houses were the emblems of the clans of those who occupied the lodges.

The old man came to a lodge on which was hung a turtle shell. Turtle Clan members lived in the house.

He pulled the door curtain and asked for food and a night's lodging.

He was refused by the woman of the house. He was told to move on.

Going on his way he soon came to a house with a snipe skin over the door.

When he asked for food,

he was again told to move on.

Thus he traveled to houses belonging to the Wolf, Beaver, Deer,

Eel, Heron, and Eagle Clans

At each house he was treated with scorn and told to move on.

At length, tired and weary, the old man came to the edge of the village. He saw a little bark house. Hanging over the door of this house was a carved bear's head. It was a house of the Bear Clan.

An old woman came out of the house. When she saw how tired the stranger looked, she asked him to enter her lodge and said that he was welcome to what little she had.

She gave him food to eat.

She spread soft deer skins and asked him to rest his tired body.

The next day the old man sickened and came down with a fever.

He told the woman to go into the forest and

36

 gather a certain kind of plant.

 He instructed her how to prepare the plant to make a certain kind of medicine.

 After taking the medicine, the old man recovered.

 The old man became ill on many different days. Each time that he was ill, it was from a different kind of sickness.

 With each illness he sent the old woman into the forest

 to gather different kinds of herbs.

 Each time that the old woman returned with the herbs, the old man gave her instructions on how to prepare and make a medicine of the herb for each kind of sickness that he had.

When he drank the medicine, he recovered.

One day the old woman was about to enter her home when she saw a great light shining in her lodge.

Upon looking up, she saw a handsome young man standing at the entrance of her bark house. His face shone like the sun.

Her heart was filled with fear. She was frightened. She thought that a spirit stood before her.

The young man said, "Fear not, good woman, I am the Creator.

"I came to the lodges of the Iroquois in the form of an old man.

"I wandered from house to house asking for food and shelter.

"I asked for food and shelter of the Turtle Clan, Snipe Clan, Wolf Clan,

"Beaver Clan, Deer Clan, Eel Clan, Heron Clan,

"and Eagle Clan. Each time I was refused food and shelter and told to move on.

"Only you, of the Bear Clan, sheltered and fed me.

'For that reason I have taught you cures for all of the sickness known to the Real People. Many times I became ill.

"Many times I sent you into the forest to gather herbs. I told you how to make medicine from the herbs."

"When I took of this medicine, I recovered from my illnesses.

"From this day on, the Medicine Men and Women will always belong to the Bear Clan.

"They, Bear Clan Members, will be the Keepers of the Medicine for all time to come."

Thunder Boy

This legend happened long ago on an island in the St. Lawrence River. The island is called by the Akwesasne Mohawks, Jo-ka-ta-ren-re, and lies opposite St. Regis Point on the St. Regis Reservation.

The story happened many summers in the past.

Long ago, a man and woman and their daughter lived alone on this island.

They had a garden where they raised corn, beans and squashes. One day, as the three were working in their garden, the sky became very dark.

Glancing up at the dark clouds,

the father said that they had better run quickly

to their house or they would be caught in the rain.

The mother shouted to her daughter, who was working at the other end of the field, telling her to cease her work and run for the house.

The man and woman then quickly ran for the house. Before they were halfway there, the storm had reached them. Heavy bursts of rain fell all about them. Flashes of lightning lit up the sky and thunder roared above them.

Inside the house, the man and woman waited for their daughter, whom they supposed was following them. "Probably when the storm overtook her, she sought shelter in the forest," said the mother. In vain, the parents waited for the daughter.

After the storm the parents returned to the field. They searched the island, but they could find no trace of the daughter. They called to the girl, but they received no answer.

Sadly they returned to their house. "The Thunder People have taken her away," said the mother, and she wept bitter tears.

The young daughter had been busy working in the garden when the storm was approaching.

43

When she saw the fast thickening clouds and heard her parents calling her to the cabin, she dropped her hoe and started to follow them.

Suddenly, she was entirely surrounded by what seemed to be a heavy mist. Her head felt strangely dizzy, and before she knew what was happening, she felt herself being lifted up into the sky. In a dazed condition, she was carried swiftly above the earth.

After awhile the girl found herself in a strange land. Never before had she seen anything like it. He, who carried her, was a little man.

He led her through this country until they came to a long council house.

Upon entering this house, the girl saw many other strange little men, all of whom stared at her. At one end of the house stood a man who seemed to be the chief of these little people.

This little chief seemed very angry when he saw the girl and her escort. "My son," said he, "Why did you bring this earth person to our country?"

The son answered, "Father, I saw her working in the field, and I fell in love with her. I wanted her, so I took her away."

The chief said, "You should have left her upon the earth. Her ways are not our ways. She cannot eat snails, bugs, and worms, which are the kinds of food that we live on."

Again he spoke, "If you insist upon keeping her here, you, yourself, must return to earth and secure earth food for her. The ways of Ra-ti-we-ras, the Thunder People, are different from the ways of the Earth People."

45

The son agreed to do this. Every day he would travel to earth to secure food for his earth wife.

For one year this earth girl lived in the country of the Thunder People. Her husband granted her every wish, and she became very happy. Though she sometimes thought of her parents, she did not become lonesome.

One day the chief of the Thunder People said, "My daughter, you are soon to give birth to a son. It would not do to have the child born in this land. You must return to your old home on the island, Jo-ka-ta-ren-re. But there is one thing I want to warn you about. After your boy is born, guard him carefully. You must warn everyone who goes near the boy never to strike him. If anyone ever strikes the boy, you will lose him."

Suddenly, without warning, the girl was again surrounded by the heavy mist. Her mind became dazed. Once again she found herself traveling at a great speed through space.

After what seemed a little while, she opened her eyes, and to her surprise, found herself in front of her mother's cabin back at the island.

The parents of the girl were happy to see her. They had long given her up for lost. The girl told her strange story and said that soon she was to give birth to a son.

What the Thunder Chief had said came true. In time a little son was born to the girl.

This boy was smaller than an earth child, and in many ways his habits differed from the habits of an ordinary boy.

Whenever a thunder storm would approach the island, the boy would become very excited. He would run out into the storm and laugh and play about.

At such times, the thunder would seem to roar more often. Great flashes of lightning would light the heavens.

The old grandmother did not like to have the boy run out into the storm.

Whenever a storm approached, she would try to shut the child up in the cabin, but the boy always managed to escape in spite of all that she could do.

One day, at the approach of a storm, the old grandmother locked the boy in the cabin.

She scolded him and forbade him to go out into the storm. The boy became very angry. He ran about the cabin, throwing to the floor everything he could get his hands on. He was in a terrible temper.

The grandmother told him to cease his mischief and to sit down, but the boy only stamped around more.

When the boy became angry, faint sounds as of distant thunder seemed to come from his body. The more angry he became, the louder the thunder sounded. His grandmother told him to cease his noise. In his rage, he continued to wreck everything he could get his hands on.

The old woman lost her temper. Taking up a stick, she gave the boy a sharp blow across his legs.

Instantly, there was a blinding flash of lightning, followed by a loud roar of thunder! The room became filled with a heavy mist.

Trembling with fear, the old woman huddled in a corner of the cabin. When the mist cleared, the boy had vanished.

Far away, she could hear a rumble of thunder, sounding fainter and fainter in the distance.

When the boy's mother returned to the cabin, she said, "you have struck my son. His father has taken him to live with him in the land of the Thunder People. We will never see him again."

Because the Thunder Boy is half Indian, the Thunder People are friends of the Indian and will never strike one of that race. In the early spring, at the coming of the first thunder, it is said to please the Thunder People if you throw real tobacco in the fire.

Note: All of the Six Nations have a similar story of the Thunder Boy.

Sa-go-ia-na-wa-sai, Our Grandfather

After Sat-kon-se-ri-io, the Good Spirit, had created the creatures of the earth, he decided to inspect his work. As he walked over the earth, he saw a stranger who was a giant with a very large ugly face. Good Spirit asked the strange being who he was. The creature answered with a roaring voice, "I am master of the earth and all things on it."

"If you are master of the earth, then the things of this earth should obey you. Let me see you show your power. Prove to me that you are what you claim to be," said Sat-kon-se-ri-io.

The monster said, "What shall be our test?" Good Spirit pointed to a distant mountain. "Can you bring that mountain to you?" he asked.

Good Spirit and the stranger turned their backs to the mountain so that they would not see it until it was near. "Mountain come here!" roared the stranger. After waiting a moment, they turned and looked at the mountain. It had not moved.

"Now it is my turn," said Good Spirit. Again they turned their backs to the mountain. Good Spirit said, "Mountain come here!" There was a roaring sound as if of a strong wind. Before the roaring sound had died away, the creature turned to look. As he did so, the onrushing mountain brushed his face. It bent his nose and twisted his mouth, and it has remained so to this very day.

The creature then said, "I now know you to be master. Command me, and your wishes will be my law."

Good Spirit said, "Because you love to wander about, it shall be your duty to travel over the earth to help mankind, whom I am about

50

to create. You will cease your evil ways and henceforth do only good."

"I will do this thing you command," said the creature who was Sa-go-ia-na-wa-sai (He Defends). "Mankind must carve a likeness of my face from living basswood trees. They must sing a song that pleases me. My spirit will enter this face. From time to time they must give me tobacco, of which I am very fond. If they follow my directions, I will be of great service to them, for my spirit and face have the power to drive away evil forces," continued Sa-go-ia-na-wa-sai.

Such is the story of Sa-go-ia-na-wa-sai, our Grandfather, he who defends us. This happened long ago when the world was young.

51

The Flying Head

This story was told me by two Oneida Indians

when I was a boy.

Many

winters

ago (arrow going back)

near Oneida Lake

there was an Oneida settlement.

In this village lived a famous Indian hunter

whose name was Wolf Marked.

Wolf Marked lived in a bark house at the edge of the village.

His only companions were two large wolf-like dogs who never left their master's side. They were his constant friends.

It was said that, while hunting, these swift running dogs would drive the game to Wolf Marked. This famous hunter was never known to have returned from the trail empty-handed.

Wolf Marked was well-liked by other members of his nation. A portion of all game brought down by his arrows was given to the needy, the widow and the orphan.

He was always ready to help those of his people who were in want or need. His aid was given willingly, and he always refused pay or reward for his services.

No one was fleeter of foot than this young man, and often the chiefs of his nation sent him with wampum messages down the long trail that bound one end of the Longhouse Country to the other. His wisdom was also great, and his advice was often asked at Council.

He was a great ball player, and many times his strong arm and fleet foot carried the ball through the goal posts of a neighboring tribe. In feats of endurance and strength, he excelled all others of his people.

One Sun (day)

Wolf Marked made preparations for a long hunt. With a new quiver of arrows and a pouch of provisions, he left the village.

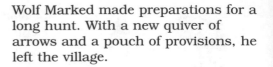

His trail led toward the west (Great Panther).

On each side of him trotted one of his faithful dogs.

All day he traveled, his eyes ever alert for signs of game. But on this day all life in the forests seemed to have vanished. Over the entire countryside a deep silence had fallen. Not a bird sang a note. Not a rabbit crossed the trail. No squirrel barked at him from the branches of a tree. Even the brook, that he occasionally crossed, refused to make a murmur. The very forest seemed to have fallen asleep. No leaf waved or rustled in the wind.

Wolf Marked was looking for signs of bear and deer.

He wondered why his two faithful dogs traveled so close to his feet. He wondered why their hair rose on their backs, why their tails lay curled beneath their bodies as if they feared something. They would sniff the air, look toward the north, and utter low and fierce growls. In this manner they traveled the entire day.

Toward sunset Wolf Marked prepared camp, making a fire and cooking their evening meal.

As Wolf Marked wondered at the strange behavior of his dogs, he thought that he heard a strange wailing cry coming from the North (Great Bear). His dogs answered by growling in their throats. He knew that they feared something very unusual.

One of the dogs got in front of his master, and looking Wolf Marked in the face, the dog spoke. "Friend," said the dog, "do not be surprised that we can speak to you in your own language. Never before have we done this, though we have the power to do so. You have been kind to us, never allowing us to go cold or hungry but always sharing with us. For that reason we are going to break our silence and warn you. A terrible monster, who is master of the forest, is coming toward your camp.

Your only hope is to run and try to reach the village clearing before the monster catches up with you. Only there can he do you no harm. Even now it may be too late for he has scented you."

There was no mistaking the terror in the eyes of his dogs. With a bound Wolf Marked flung his pack aside and ran down the trail toward the village, his dogs following close behind him.

He knew his only hope for life was to reach the clearing that surrounded his village.

As Wolf Marked ran, he heard again the terrible wail of the monster. It was a high, long, drawn out, piercing wail. It was a cry that Wolf Marked had never heard before. Sometimes it reminded him of the scream of a mountain lion. Again, it resembled the howl of a wolf or the roar of the north wind, screaming through the forest. As Wolf Marked ran, the wail got nearer and nearer. The creature was fast gaining on him.

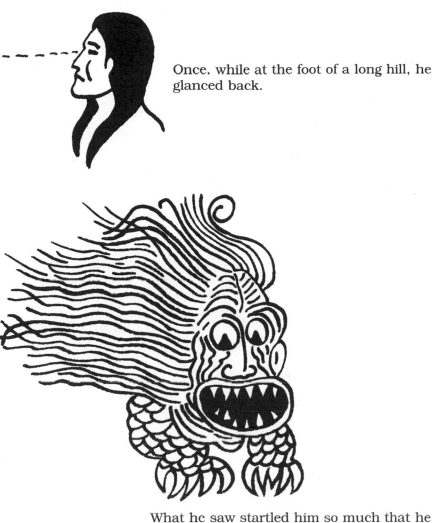

Once. while at the foot of a long hill, he glanced back.

What he saw startled him so much that he almost froze in his tracks. For a moment he could not run. A great fiery head with large, round, yellow eyes, a long hooked beak, and large open mouth appeared over the brow of the hill. The creature had fiery hair that flowed in a long wavy streak as the monster traveled. It had no body, but fastened to the bottom of the huge head were two, scale-covered paws, on the ends of which were long curved, ugly-looking claws.

The monster traveled in a peculiar fashion. It would jump to the foot of a tree, climb the tree, and then bound to the foot of another tree. In this way it traveled very rapidly. There was a wide burnt path, cutting back through the forest where the creature had traveled.

Soon Wolf Marked could feel the hot breath of the creature on the back of his neck. One of his dogs spoke to him, saying, "Brother, the creature is almost upon us. I am going back to fight it. I can delay it for a little while, but I will never see you again on this earth. Farewell, kind and good friend." Saying this, the dog turned and ran back.

Wolf Marked heard barking and growling and then a yelp of pain. He knew that his faithful dog was dead and was being eaten by the Head. His friend had given his life for him.

Wolf Marked ran on. The village was just around the bend of a hill. If he could only make it, he knew that he would be safe. Again he heard the wailing cry of the creature. Nearer and nearer it sounded. He could feel the hot breath of the head singe his head hair. Sparks from its fiery mouth fell around him. The monster was close.

His brave dog fell behind him, getting between the Monster and Wolf Marked.

The remaining dog said, "Brother, the creature is almost upon us. Perhaps I can delay it until you reach the village. I am going back to fight it. I will never see you again on this earth. Farewell, kind and faithful friend."

Saying this, the dog turned and ran back over the trail. Wolf Marked heard barking and growling and then a yelp of pain. He knew that his faithful friend was dead and was being eaten by the monster.

He was tired but ran on, and after a brief silence, he again heard the wail of the monster. He could hear the creature getting nearer as it cut a burning path through the forest. He could feel the hot breath burn his back. He could sense its huge eyes upon him.

Ahead of him he could see the sky lit up by the fires of the village.

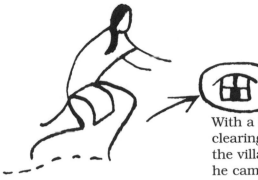

With a staggering run, he entered the clearing in the center of which was the village. Running across the field he came to a stop and, with his startled people, looked back over his trail.

A great head came bounding up to the edge of the forest. Showers of sparks shot from its mouth. Its great yellow eyes glared in fiery hatred at the people. With a mighty bound and a terrible cry of anger, it turned and disappeared over the dark forest, traveling toward the North.

In ancient days, this story was told to show the fidelity of the dog. It was and is a belief of the Old People that a person who was cruel to dogs could never reach the Land of Happy Spirits.

The Fierce Beast

This story was told me by De-ha-we-ia-he-le (David Hill), a Mohawk of Six Nations country, Ohsweken, Ontario, Canada.

In ancient days three brothers were camped beside a mountain in what is now New York State. They were on a hunting trip and had left their main village on the Mohawk River.

One morning the oldest brother took his bow and quiver of arrows and, stepping into the forest, said that he was going to hunt for deer. He told his two brothers to remain in camp until his return.

The hunter did not return, and after waiting two days, the next older brother said that he would see if he could get a deer. He said he would find the missing brother. Taking his bow and arrows, he went into the forest.

The little brother waited patiently for his two brothers to return. After waiting for two days, the little boy finished eating the last of the supply of meat that was in camp. He knew that if he did not get any fresh meat that he would starve to death. So, taking his bow and arrows, he also went into the forest.

After wandering for several hours, he came to a little stream. "Here," thought he, "I will find game of some kind." Quietly he followed the course of the brook, his sharp eyes watching for a rabbit or a squirrel. The stream wound in and out among the trees. The little boy followed the winding stream for some time. The stream led the boy to a beautiful valley surrounded by high hills.

As the boy wandered on up this valley, he happened to look up at one of the hills that overshadowed the stream. At the foot of this hill he saw a cave. "Perhaps I will find game in the cave," thought he. He left the flat land, and, climbing to the entrance of the cave, he glanced in.

The inside of the cave was very dark, but the little boy was very brave. Firmly grasping his bow and an arrow, he crept into the dark shadows. For awhile he could see where he was going, but, as he went farther back from the mouth of the cave, it became very dark. In a little while he could see nothing at all, but still he walked on. As he was groping his way into the heart of the hill, he stepped into a huge hole in the floor of the cave. Without warning, he fell into a deep pit. He felt himself falling down, down, he knew not where. Every minute he expected to crash against the ragged rocks at the bottom of the pit, but, to his surprise, he continued falling.

After falling for what seemed a long time, the boy saw far below him a pinhole of light. As he fell toward this light, it became brighter and larger until he saw that it was an opening in the bottom of the pit. Below the opening was a body of water that seemed to be a lake. As the boy fell through the hole, he braced his body for a plunge into the water. Down he fell into the lake. Gasping for breath, the boy swam up until his head was above water. Near at hand was land, and, as he was a good swimmer, he soon reached shore.

Stepping upon a sandy beach, he found himself in a strange country. The grass was so big that he had to walk around each blade. A blade of grass was higher than a tree. Flowers towered high above his head. The little boy came to what he thought was a cliff. Upon walking around the edge of it, he found it to be a tree. The top branches were so high that he could not see them. An ant hill was as high as a mountain in this strange country.

The little boy still held his bow and arrows and now, very cautiously, stalked around the tall grass. He came to a little hill and was just about to climb it when he heard voices on the other side. Grasping his hunting knife, he slowly crept toward the sound. Cautiously walking from behind a blade of grass, the little boy saw his two missing brothers.

The two brothers appeared very excited and were looking up at the branches of a gigantic tree. The little brother went to them. He asked them why they were so excited.

"Look at that great animal in the tree," said the older brother. "We have been trying for several days to kill it. If we could kill it and bring its great skin back to the village, we would be greatly honored." Saying this, he shot an arrow at the fierce monster.

Glancing up, the little brother saw a fierce looking animal crouched on a large branch of the tree. As the little brother looked up, the arrow that the older brother had just shot struck the tail of the monster. With a deafening roar, the huge creature jumped down on the branch below him. The fierce animal glared down at the three brothers and, opening his mouth, showed its great teeth, at the same time letting out a roar, which could be heard for many miles around. The two other brothers had exhausted their supply of arrows and, turning to the little brother, asked him for his quiver of arrows. They then shot arrow after arrow at the huge beast. Occasionally an arrow would hit a limb of the tree or glance off the monster's thick hide. At such times the beast would growl and jump to a lower branch, getting nearer and nearer to the three brothers.

Finally, there was but one arrow left, and the creature was still alive. The little brother then said, "Let me try. Perhaps I can hit him," and, taking up the last arrow, he carefully drew it to its head. Taking very careful aim, he let the arrow fly. Up, up it went and with a thud, cut through the beast's thick hide and into its heart!

With a deafening roar, the giant creature pawed the air, lost its balance, and fell crashing to the earth. Over and over, it fell, breaking the heavy branches of the tree as if they were spider's webs. Down he fell, straight at the boys, who jumped to one side and hid behind three blades of grass. With a loud thump, the monster fell on its back, the earth trembling as he hit the ground.

Eagerly the brothers rushed out from behind the grass. They stared in awe at such a gigantic monster. Never before had they seen such a big creature. "The meat will last for many days," said little brother. "It will take all three of us to carry its huge hide," said oldest brother. "We are great hunters," said middle brother.

The brothers grasped the legs of the monster and tried to pull it over on its side. They pulled and pulled and, exerting all of their combined strength, they managed to pull the giant animal over.

What do you think it was???

Answer — A mouse!!!!

The Discovery of Fire, A Tradition

In olden times when a Mohawk boy had reached the age of 14 winters (years), it was customary for him to make a journey, accompanied by his father, to some sacred place back up in the mountains. There, after receiving instructions from his father, the youth would remain alone for at least four days. During these four or more days, the Mohawk boy would perform a ceremony known as the Dream Fast. This Dream Fast was very important to the Indian boy of long ago. To be successful in the Dream Fast meant that the Indian was no longer a youth but a man. During the fast, the Clan Spirit of the young Mohawk would appear to him in a dream and reveal to him the bird, animal or plant that was to be the Mohawk's guardian throughout his life. After the fast he must secure something from the creature of his dream and must wear it in his medicine bag as a sort of a charm.

The Mohawk Iroquois had three clans: the Bear clan, Turtle Clan, and Wolf Clan. Should the dreamer belong to the Turtle Clan, the Spirit of the turtle would appear to him in a dream and show him his future guardian. If the clan spirit did not appear to him during the feast, his father, who visited him daily, released him, and he departed home, a failure. He could not have two chances. The dreamer could leave his fasting place after sunset for brief periods. He could drink water to quench his thirst. He was not allowed to eat any food.

Otjiera belonged to the Bear Clan and was the son of a famous leader. He had many honors to his credit. No youth of the Mohawks was fleeter on foot than he. He led in the games and was one of the best lacrosse players of his nation.

He could shoot his arrow farther and straighter than any of his friends. He knew the forest and streams and would always return from the hunt loaded down with deer meat, which he always divided with the needy of his people. He could imitate the calls of the birds. They would come when he called and would sit on his shoulders. He was the pride of his people.

The time for the Dream Fast of Otjiera had come. It was in the Moon of Strawberries. Otjiera was eager to try the test of strength and endurance. High upon the mountain, on a huge ledge of rock, he built his lodge of young saplings. He covered it with the branches of the balsam to shelter it from the rains. He removed all of his clothing save his breech cloth and moccasins. Appealing to his clan spirit, he entered the crude shelter.

Four suns had passed, and yet the young warrior had not been visited by the clan spirit. The fifth sun had dawned when his father appeared. He shook the lodge poles and called for Otjiera to come forth.

Otjiera in a low and weak voice begged his father to give him one more day. His father left, telling Otjiera that on the morrow he must return to his village.

That night Otjiera looked down from his lodge on the mountains. In the distance he heard low rumblings of thunder. As he listened the thunder became louder and louder. Bright flashes of lightning lit up the heavens.

"Great Thunder Man, Ra-ti-we-ras," prayed the youth, "Send my Clan Spirit to help me." He had no sooner spoken than a blinding flash of lightning lit the sky and a rumble of thunder shook the mountain top. Otjiera looked and beheld his clan spirit. A huge bear stood beside him in his lodge. Suddenly the bear spoke, "This night, Otjiera, you shall have a magic that will not only aid you, but will also aid all of the Ongwe-Oweh, the Real People (Indians)."

There was a blinding flash of lightning and Otjiera awoke from his vision. He rubbed his eyes and looked for the clan spirit. The bear was gone. The youth wondered what his guardian helper would be. He looked out from his lodge. The storm had not yet left the mountain. Suddenly he heard a strange sound outside nearer the lodge! It was a dreadful screeching sound such as he had never heard before. He wondered what kind of animal or bird made such a dreadful noise. The sound had ceased. Then, almost over his head, he saw the cause of the sound. The wind was causing two balsam trees to rub their branches against each other. As the wood rubbed, the friction caused the strange, screeching sound. As Otjiera watched, he saw a strange thing happen. The strong wind, rushing up the mountain, caused the trees to bend and sway more rapidly. When the two trees rubbed against each other, a thin string of smoke appeared. As the boy watched, the wood burst into flame.

Otjiera was, at first, frightened. He started to run. None of his people had ever seen fire so near, and it was feared. The boy remembered his clan spirit. "This must be what the great bear meant," thought the boy.

That day Otjiera took two pieces of dry balsam wood. He rubbed the wood together as he had seen the storm do the night before. He soon tired and was about to throw the wood away when he noticed a thin thread of smoke coming from the wood. He rubbed harder and soon a tiny spark appeared. By using some dry cedar bark and grass he soon had a fire.

When his father and two chiefs came that noon, they found a happy Otjiera. He had a very powerful helper, a strong medicine which afterwards was to help all of his people. That was how fire came to the Indian people of long ago.

The Invention of the Bow and Arrow

Long ago the Indian people did not have the bow and arrow for a weapon. At that time, a spear was the common weapon used in the hunt.

One day a young Indian hunter, whose name was Ohgweluhndoe, left his village in search of a bear. His only weapon was a long spear, tipped with flint. Ohgweluhndoe walked a long way. He saw no signs of bear. After a while, the thought came to him that perhaps he would find a bear in a thickly forested glen that was not far away. In this particular place there were wild grape vines. It was at the time of the Moon of Falling Leaves (October). The grapes would be ripe and the bear would, no doubt, be eating them.

Ohgweluhndoe was not wrong in his guess. As he entered the thickest part of the glen, he caught sight of a huge black figure. It was Ohgwali, the bear, and he was busy eating wild grapes. From time to time, he would grunt little squeals of pleasure as he gulped the wild grapes down. The young hunter crept very close. He was almost within reach of the bear. Quietly he raised the spear for the death stroke, and (that) would have materialized but for one thing. As Ohgweluhndoe was about to throw the spear, his foot slipped on a rock, and he fell sprawling to the ground, almost under the bear's claws. With a startled grunt the hunter looked up. He still held the spear, but now he was in no position to throw it. Oh-gwa-li, the bear, ordinarily would have run away from a human hunter; but the sudden appearance of the young Indian startled him, and instead of running away as most black bears do, he turned and started for the hunter. Ohgweluhndoe did not take long in getting to his feet. With one jump he was on his feet and, in a moment, was heading through the forest. The bear, seeing that the hunter was running from him, gained courage and quickly took after Ohgweluhndoe. For a short while the two, the hunter and the bear, kept the same speed, but in a short time the bear gained rapidly on the hunter.

Ohgweluhndoe knew that in a very little while the bear would have him and that probably he would be torn to pieces. He thought of his wife and son waiting for his return. This thought made him determined to kill the bear or die in the attempt. Turning quickly, he made ready to throw his spear, but the end of the spear had caught on a twisted grape vine, which was clinging to the top of a small ash sapling. The hunter tried to pull the spear free from the vine, but he only succeeded in bending the sapling. The bear was almost upon the Indian. Ohgweluhndoe made one more effort to pull the spear loose. As he tugged at the spear, he pulled the sapling to the ground. He did not wait long. With a startled yell, he let the spear go and turned to run. He did not run many steps when he noticed that the bear was not following him. He looked back. The bear was on the ground with the spear stuck through his neck. The blood was rapidly reddening the leaves as Ohgwali gave a few final kicks before death came. The surprised hunter went back to see what had happened. The spear which had caught on the vine had caused the sapling to bend, thus forming a bow. The vine had been the bow string, the sapling the bow. When the hunter had pulled the spear, he had caused the sapling to bend. When he dropped the spear, the sapling had sprung upright again. The force of this spring had whipped the vine straight, at the same time, throwing the spear ahead into Ohgwali's neck.

The hunter again took the spear and put the end of it on the vine. Pulling the vine back, he bent the sapling. When the sapling had bent almost to the ground, he released the spear. It shot through the air. Thus, the bow was invented.

In time the Indians made smaller bows out of smaller saplings. Instead of a grapevine bow string they used one of rawhide. Instead of a heavy spear, they used an arrow, tipped with flint and winged with feathers. The bow became a priceless weapon for the Indian people of long ago.

The Rabbit Dance

In a wild section of the Adirondack Mountains, there camped a hunting party of Mohawk Indians. During the Leaf-Falling Moon (October), many of the Mohawks left their main villages along the Mohawk River and traveled north to the mountains where the hunting was good. There, in the heavily forested mountain valleys, the hunters would store up deer meat and deer skins for winter use. When a goodly supply had been gathered the people followed the hunting trails south to the main Mohawk settlements. Some of the hunters usually remained in the mountains during the winter months because of the good trapping of fur-bearing animals in that region. Beaver skins were valuable for trade even before the white man came with his guns and fire-water to exchange for them.

In this particular hunting camp lived two little Indian boys. One was called Hot-no-wah, the Turtle, and the other was nicknamed Oweya, the Wing.

Early one morning while the hunters were making preparations for a deer drive, the Turtle and Wing set out on a little exploring trip of their own. In their hands they carried their little bows. A quiver of arrows was strapped across each of their backs. The little boys walked on and on through the forest. They walked silently and were very careful not to make any noise, for their eyes were on the lookout for game. Perhaps they could surprise a chipmunk or a squirrel. After walking quite a distance from camp, they came to a little clearing in the pines. As they approached this clearing, they noticed little trails or paths running into it. These, they knew, were rabbit runways, so they tightened their grip on their bows and were more on the alert for game. The boys walked to the center of the clearing and looked around for rabbits.

Suddenly, there was a loud thumping sound. It seemed to come from the ground. Looking ahead, the boys, to their amazement, saw a huge brown rabbit. The huge creature was as large as the boys. It stood for a few moments looking at the little Mohawks. Turtle and Wing forgot all about hunting rabbits. Never before had they seen such a huge rabbit. At first they were frightened, but, as the rabbit made no move to harm them, their fears left them.

After looking the boys over, the rabbit again thumped the ground with his hind legs. Immediately a long line of rabbits appeared, running rapidly down one of the runways. Quickly they approached the clearing where, to the surprise of the two boys, they performed all sorts of queer antics. There seemed to be hundreds of rabbits. There was an endless line of rabbits, running, hopping, skipping and chasing each other down the narrow rabbit path and into the clearing. They seemed to be everywhere and all were very frolicsome as they hopped and skipped about. Sometimes they seemed to be playing the game, "Follow the Leader."

They ran here and there, several in a line, all following one rabbit. Occasionally they ran in circles, hopping and kicking as they went. Meanwhile, the large chief rabbit remained near the boys. He watched his lively tribe, but in no way did he take part in the rabbit games except to stand guard.

As the boys watched the rabbits skip and hop around them, they forgot their fear of the big chief rabbit. Boy-like they wanted to play tag with the rabbits. Turtle made a grab for one of the rabbits, and when he missed him, set out in pursuit. Wing forgot the big chief rabbit and joined the chase.

Without warning a loud Thump! Thump! Thump! was heard. The big chief rabbit was warning his tribe. Immediately, every rabbit stopped still in his tracks! They seemed to be frozen to the ground, so motionless did they become. The now startled boys ceased their running and gazed in fright at the big rabbit. The chief rabbit gave two more thumps. Immediately, the other rabbits jumped into action!

Following each other single file, they left the clearing and disappeared up the runway from where they had come.

The big chief rabbit waited until the last rabbit had left the clearing. Then, giving a final thump, he too hopped up the rabbit trail and was soon lost to view.

The two boys were very surprised at what they had seen. Quickly they returned to the hunting camp where they told their father what they had seen. Their father laughed and said that they were good story tellers. But their wise old grandfather said that the boys were fortunate to have seen what had happened.

"You saw the Rabbit Dance," said he. "The rabbits, like the Indians, have their own trails and their own council ground. They hold councils and move from place to place. They have secret signals which are given by thumps on the ground with their hind legs. Very few people have seen the Rabbit Dance, and those who are so fortunate as to have seen it, usually become very good hunters. The big rabbit that you saw was the big chief rabbit, and he was watching over his people," and the old man wisely shook his head as he went into the bark house.

The Story of
The Great Bear,
The Big Dipper

This is a story that old Iroquois told to their children during the winter moons (months).

Many (a heap) winters (years)

in the past (arrow going backward),

there was a Mohawk village of bark houses along the Oswego River.

One day Mohawk hunters discovered the tracks of a giant bear.

After that they saw the tracks many times. Sometimes the tracks would circle the Indian village.

The game began to disappear from the forests, and the Mohawks knew that the giant bear was killing and carrying off all of the game.

Because of scarcity of game, famine came to the Mohawks. The meat racks were empty. The people were hungry. Starvation faced them.

The head chief said, "We must kill this giant bear who is causing all of our trouble."

At once a party of warriors set out in search of the bear. They soon came upon his tracks in the snow. They followed the bear tracks for many days.

They finally came upon the huge beast.

At once the air was filled with the arrows of the warriors.

To the surprise and dismay of the Mohawks, the arrows failed to pierce the thick hide of the bear. Many broken arrows fell from his tough skin.

At last the angry bear turned and charged the hunters, who fled but were soon overtaken. Most of them were killed.

Only two hunters escaped, and they returned to the village to tell the sad tale.

The two hunters told the council of the Great Bear.

They told what had happened to the war-party.

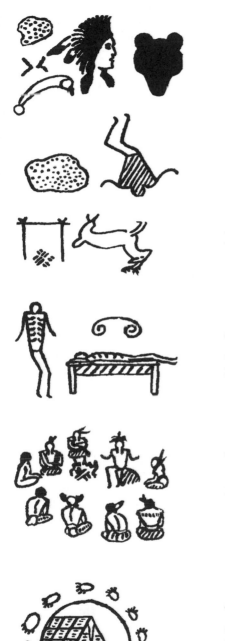

Party after party of warriors set out to destroy the Great Bear, but always they failed. There were many battles fought between the bear and the warriors.

Many warriors were slain.

As time went on, more and more deer vanished from the forest. The smoking racks were empty.

The people became very thin because of the lack of food. Starvation caused many to become sick.

The people were filled with fear, and their hungry bodies crept close to the fire at night.

They feared the Great Bear, whose giant tracks circled their town each night.

They feared to leave their village because they could hear, coming from the darkness of the forest, the loud cough of the Great Bear.

One night three brothers each had a strange dream. On three successive nights they had the same vision.

They dreamed that they had tracked and killed the Great Bear.

They said, "The dream must be true."

So getting their weapons and a scanty supply of food, they set out after the bear. In a little while they came upon the tracks of the great beast. Quickly they followed the trail, their arrows ready.

For many moons they followed the tracks of the bear across the earth.

The tracks led them to the end of the world. Looking ahead, they saw the giant beast leap from the earth into the heavens. The three hunters soon came to the jumping-off place.

Without hesitation the three of them followed the bear into the sky. There in the heavens you can see them chasing the bear during the long winter nights.

In the fall of the year when the bear gets ready to sleep for the winter,

the three hunters get near enough to shoot their arrows into his body.

His dripping blood, caused by the wounds from the arrows, turn the autumn leaves red and yellow. But he always manages to escape from the hunters. For a time, after being wounded, he is invisible. Afterwards he reappears.

When the Iroquois see the Big Dipper in the sky, they say, "See, the three hunters are still chasing the Great Bear."

Why We Have Mosquitoes

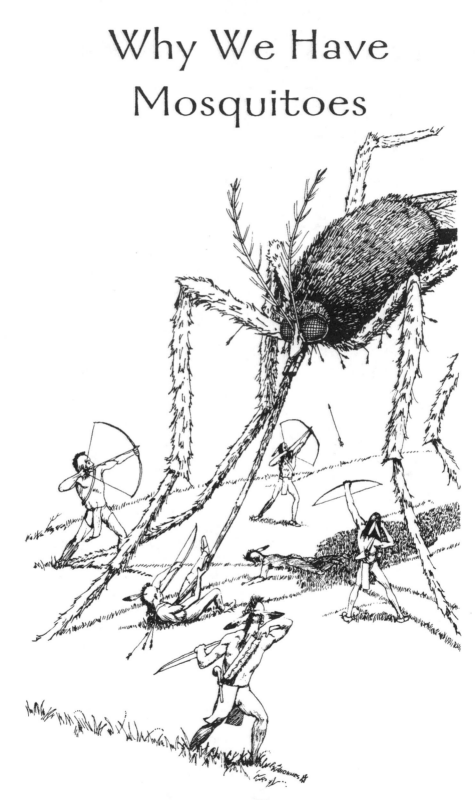

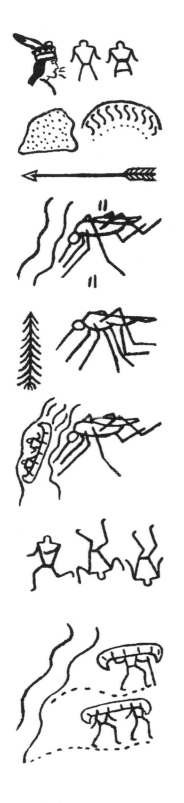

The old Iroquois Indians used to tell this story to the children:

Many winters

in the past

two giant mosquitoes appeared on either side of a river.

These giant creatures were as tall as a good-sized pine tree.

As the Indian people paddled down the river in their canoes, these giant creatures would bend their heads and attack them with their giant beaks.

The mosquitoes killed many people.

Knowing that these giant mosquitoes were waiting to attack any canoe that floated down the river, the people began to shun that particular stream.

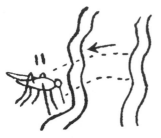

It was then that these giant creatures moved to other streams to seek their prey.

For a time, it was a reign of terror for the Iroquois who were great canoe travelers. They never knew just when these giant mosquitoes would pounce upon and devour them.

Finally, in desperation, a war party was organized to seek out these creatures and destroy them.

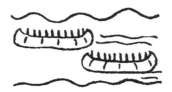

Twenty warriors in two great canoes floated down a river where they expected the mosquitoes to be.

In their hands, ever ready, they held their bows and arrows.

Fastened to their belts were their war clubs and hunting knives.

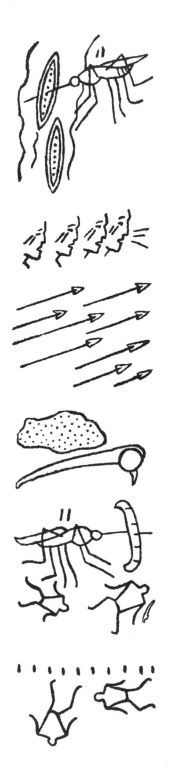

Suddenly, two huge shadows loomed over them and a giant beak pierced one of the canoes.

Giving their war cry, the warriors filled the air

with many arrows.

The battle was terrific!

The giant mosquitoes seemed to be everywhere at the same time.

In a little while half of the warriors had been killed.

The remaining braves determined to die courageously.

Singing their Death Song, they attacked the huge creatures on land.

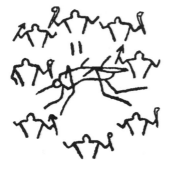

They hid behind the trees and bushes.

They surrounded the mosquitoes, who were unable to get at them because of the thick branches.

The Iroquois buried many of their arrows in the bodies of the two mosquitoes.

Finally, after most of the arrows had been shot and the supply was very low, the two mosquitoes fell to the earth, covered with many wounds.

Immediately, the warriors fell upon them with their war clubs and, with powerful blows, tore their bodies apart.

From the blood of the two big mosquitoes there sprang many little mosquitoes, and the air was filled with them. These little mosquitoes, like their grandfathers, are fond of the taste of human blood. They hate man for killing their grandfathers and are continually trying to get revenge upon man for this reason. That is how mosquitoes came to be. The battles between man and the mosquitoes took place upon Seneca River in New York State.

Song of the Hermit Thrush

Long ago the birds had no songs. Only man could sing and every morning man would greet the rising sun with a song. The birds, as they were flying by, would often stop and listen to the beautiful songs of man. In their hearts they wished that they too could sing. One day the Good Spirit visited the earth.

The Good Spirit walked over the earth inspecting the various things that he had created. As he walked through the forest, he noticed that there was a great silence. Something seemed to be missing

As the Good Spirit pondered, the sun sank behind the western hills. From the direction of the river, where an Indian village was, there sounded the deep, rich tones of an Indian drum, followed by the sacred chanting of the sunset song. The Good Spirit listened. The song was pleasing to the ears of the Good Spirit.

The Good Spirit looked around. He noticed that the birds were also listening to the singing. "That is what is missing", said the Good Spirit, "Birds should have songs."

The next day the Good Spirit called all of the birds to a great council. From near and far they came. The sky was filled with flying birds.

The trees and bushes bent to the earth under the weight of so many.

On the great Council Rock sat the Good Spirit. He waited until all of the birds had perched and had become quiet.

The Good Spirit spoke. He asked the birds if they would like to have songs, songs such as the People sang.

With one accord, the birds all chirped, "Yes, yes!"

"Very well," said the Good Spirit, "Tomorrow when the sun rises in the east, you are all to fly up in the sky. You are to fly as high as you can. When you can fly no higher, you will find your song. That bird who flies the highest will have the most beautiful song of all the birds." Saying these words the Good Spirit vanished.

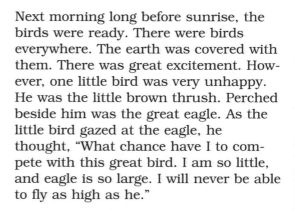

Next morning long before sunrise, the birds were ready. There were birds everywhere. The earth was covered with them. There was great excitement. However, one little bird was very unhappy. He was the little brown thrush. Perched beside him was the great eagle. As the little bird gazed at the eagle, he thought, "What chance have I to compete with this great bird. I am so little, and eagle is so large. I will never be able to fly as high as he."

As he was thus thinking, an idea entered his mind, "Eagle is so excited that he will not notice me." With this thought in mind, the little brown bird flew like a flash to the eagle's head and quickly hid under his feathers. The great eagle was so excited that he did not notice the little thrush. "With my great wings, I will surely win," thought he.

The sun finally looked over the eastern hill. With a great roar of wings, the many birds took off.

The air was so full of flying birds that for a time the sky was dark. Their bodies covered the face of the sun.

For a long time the birds flew upward. Finally the smaller, weaker, birds began to tire. The hummingbird was the first to give up. His little wings beat the air so hard that to this day one can, if one listens, hear his humming wings. His little squeaky call says, "Wait, wait for me," a very plain song.

The fat cowbird was the next to give up. As he floated down, he listened and heard his song, a very common song. Other birds weakened and while flying earthward, listened and learned their songs.

At last the sun was at the end of the earth. The night sky began to darken the earth. By this time there were only a few birds left. They were the larger, strong winged birds, the eagle, hawk, buzzard and loon. All night the birds flew up, ever up.

When the sun rose next morning only the eagle, chief of all birds, was left. He was still going strong.

When the sun was halfway in the sky, he began to tire. Finally with a look of triumph, for there were no other birds in sight, the tired eagle began to soar earthward. The little thrush, riding under the feathers of the great eagle, had been asleep all of this time. When the eagle started back to earth, little thrush awoke. He hopped off the eagle's head and began to fly upward. Eagle saw him go and glared with anger at him but was powerless to stop him, as he was completely exhausted.

The little thrush flew up and up. He soon came to a hole in the sky. He found himself in a beautiful country, the Happy Hunting Grounds. As he entered the Spirit World, he heard a beautiful song.

He stayed in heaven awhile, learning this song.

When he learned it completely, he left the Land of Happy Spirits and flew back toward earth.

Thrush could hardly wait to reach the earth. He was anxious to show off his beautiful song.

As thrush neared the earth, he glanced down at the Council Rock. There sat all of the birds, and on the Council Rock, glaring up at him was Akwcks, the eagle. All the birds were silent, as they waited for thrush to light on the council ground.

Suddenly, the feeling of glory left the little thrush and he felt ashamed. He knew that he had cheated to get his beautiful song. He also feared Akweks, who might get even with him for stealing a free ride. He flew in silence to the deep woods and in shame, with dragging heart, hid under the branches of the largest tree. He was so ashamed that he wanted no one to see him.

There you will find him today. Never does the Hermit Thrush come out in the open. He is still ashamed because he cheated. Sometimes, however, he cannot restrain himself, and he must sing his beautiful song. When he does this, the other birds cease their singing. Well they know that the song of the Hermit Thrush, the song from heaven, will make their songs sound very weak. That is why Hermit Thrush is so shy. That is why his song is the most beautiful song of all of the birds. That is why this spirit song causes the sun to shine in the hearts of the Indian people, who hear it as they go into the dark forest.

The old Six Nations People told this story to their children to teach them to be honest, that it does not pay to cheat.

The Seven Dancers

Many winters

in the past (arrow going back)

the Mohawk Nation (People of the Flint)

were camped

on the Lake Keniatiio (pronounced Kahn-yah-DEE-yo) *(Lake Ontario)*.

At that time, a group of children, seven in number, formed a secret organization among themselves.

In the night

they would gather around their little council fire in the forest near the lake. There they would dance to the beat of their leader's water drum.

One day

their little chief suggested that they hold a feast

at their next council fire.

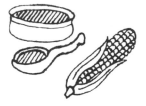

Each of the seven boys was to ask his mother for some food to take to the feast.

One boy was to ask for corn soup. One was to ask for deer meat. Another was to ask for green corn and so on.

The next day

each boy approached his mother and asked for the desired food. Each of the boys was refused the food. Each mother told her son that he had enough to eat at home, and that there was no need for him to carry away good food to the woods for a feast.

The little warriors were very unhappy because of their failure to secure food for the feast. They had empty hands and gloomy hearts.

That night they returned to the dancing ground.

The little chief said, "Never mind, my warriors. We will show our parents that it is not well to refuse us food. We will dance without our feast."

The little chief told his warriors to dance hard. He told them to look up at the sky while they danced. The chief told them not to look back, even though their parents might call for them to return.

Saying this, he took his water drum and, while beating it, he sang a very powerful song, a witch song.

The boys danced, and as they danced, their hearts became light. They soon forgot their troubles.

Faster went the song, and soon the boys began to feel themselves dance into the sky.

Their parents saw them dancing above the tree tops, and called for them to return.

One little dancer looked back,

and he became a shooting star.

The rest of the dancers became little flickering stars in the skies.

When the Mohawks see the Pleiades flickering and dancing during the cold winter nights, they say:

"The little warriors are dancing hard tonight."

Forever they dance

over the villages of the Iroquois. When they dance directly overhead, it is time for

the Iroquois New Year Feast.

This happens during the Moon (month) of the New Year, in January or February.

When a meteor falls through the sky, the Old People tell this story to the children.

Tehanetorens
(Ray Fadden)

Imagine. Imagine waiting on the shoreline watching approaching vessels. Imagine standing beside the rivers, on the hillsides, mountains, and mesas watching the unending line, the swarm of alien peoples. Imagine the stories which must have arisen to explain the coming of these people. How could the Original Peoples of this land have explained the waves of military invasions, missionaries, traders, and settlers, all of whom changed the land? How could they have explained the proliferation of diseases against which ancient ceremonies and healing rituals were powerless? As all people must, the Onkwehonwe, the Original Peoples, created and recreated themselves in story.

In the late 19th and early 20th centuries, interest in Iroquois stories focussed on collecting the stories in anticipation of the complete disappearance of Iroquoian peoples into the American mainstream. Not until Ray Fadden began his work in the 1930s

was there an active attempt to learn the stories and lifeways of the Iroquois in order for Iroquois young people to understand the ways of their ancestors. The stories Fadden was able to collect can be heard and seen in the collective artistry of Tehanetorens (Ray Fadden), his son and daughter-in-law, John (Kahionhes) and Eva Fadden, and their children, Don, David and Dan. *Legends of the Iroquois* contains a selection of works included in the Six Nations Educational Cultural Series published by Ray Fadden in the 1930s and '40s.

Fadden was fascinated by Native American cultures from the beginning. As a young man he hitchhiked from one Iroquois community to another in search of elders from whom he could learn the tribal lore which would enable him to present culturally relevant materials through the school system. A graduate of Fredonia Normal School (now State University of New York at Fredonia), his teaching career began on the Tuscarora Reservation in Sanborn, New York. There he was fortunate to meet and marry Christine Chubb of Akwesasne (St. Regis Mohawk Reservation). Without the support and encouragement of Christine, Ray's vision of an appropriate education for Native American children could not have been fulfilled. Once the Faddens returned to Akwesasne and Ray joined the faculty of the St. Regis Mohawk School, he attempted to implement his culturally relevant education for Mohawk students, education which would encourage pride in Iroquoian ancestry. However, the administrators responsible for the formal schooling of Akwesasne Mohawk students did not share Fadden's vision.

To understand how remarkable it is that Ray Fadden was able to implement his vision of what education could be, it is necessary to know some of the historical context. From the start, New York State's educational policy relating to Indian people was inseparable from non-Native political and religious interests. Missionaries established mission schools in order to Christianize Native Americans, and the educational curriculum of those schools was designed for that purpose. When the primary interest of the government became assimilation, school curriculum emphasized vocational training. But Native people actively opposed assimilation. When New York State assumed responsibility for the education of Iroquoian children in 1846, it had become apparent that not all Native American people were going to become completely assimilated. Iroquoian resistance to assimilation was characterized as resistance to formal schooling. In their introduction to *Indian Education in New York State, 1846-1953-54*, a 1959 report by Ruth A. Birdseye, Walter A. LeBaron, Chief of the Bureau of Elementary School Supervision, and Ronald P. Daly, Supervisor of Elementary Education, said that "The efforts of the state to bring equal educational opportunities to all children regardless of race, creed, or color, though never forsaken, met with almost insurmountable difficulties when applied to the education of Indian children." The "insurmountable difficulties" resulted because the State legislature wanted to separate children from the influence of their families and communities for as long as possible. According to Birdseye, "It was the intent of the legislature that the Indian child be taken at an early age from home and placed under the wholesome influence of school and teacher." The legislature also required more years of schooling and a longer school year for each reservation child than for any other children in the state.

Although New York State had passed compulsory education laws on

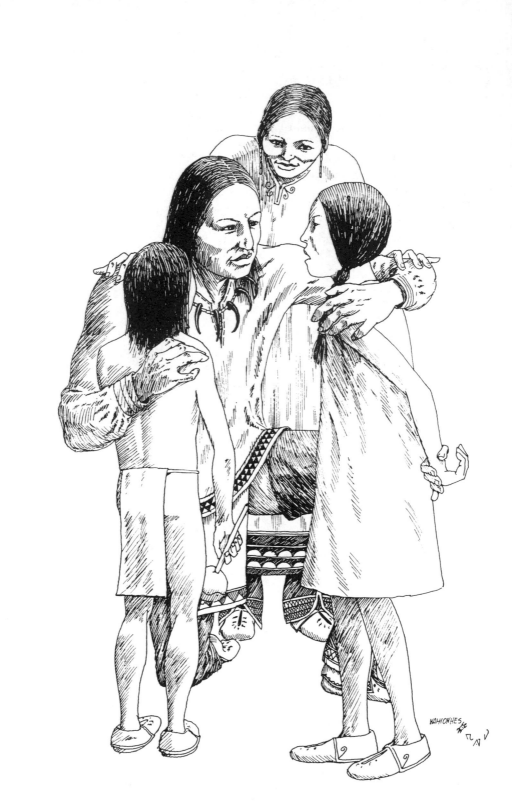

Indian reservations, the laws could not be enforced because Indian people, as citizens of independent nations, chose to resist compulsory education based on their treaty rights. There were good reasons for Akwesasne residents to resent formal schooling. In an article written in 1963, Harriet H. Shoen recalled the social and educational restrictions affecting teachers at Akwesasne in 1915. According to Shoen, teachers were to restrict their teaching vocabulary to 300 words, were not to allow Indian children to speak their Indian language either in the school buildings or on the school grounds, were not to fraternize with adult Indians, were not to stay overnight in an Indian home, and were not allowed to marry an Indian. State law required children between the ages of six and sixteen to attend schools or alternative instruction in which "at least the common school branches of reading, spelling, writing, arithmetic, English grammar, and geography are taught . . ." (Birdseye, 1959). Penalties under this act, imposed on parents or guardians not requiring children to attend school, included fines and imprisonment, but the compulsory education law continued to be resisted and remained largely unenforceable until 1924. In that year Congress passed Chapter 233-An Act to authorize the Secretary of the Interior to issue certificates of citizenship to Indians. As citizens, Indians could now be compelled to attend school.

Government schools provided a grammar school education at best, which Native American people had come to realize did not prepare them to compete economically with their peers educated in white schools. Now that barriers to the enforcement of compulsory education for Indian children had been overcome, and attendance by reservation children increased, the inadequacies of the schools to meet the needs of Indian children began to be officially acknowledged. In the 1930s, Ray Fadden recognized intuitively the need to incorporate culturally relevant material into the reservation school curriculum, but he was not able to persuade local principals. Even the New York State Education Department was thwarted in its attempt to improve educational services to Native children. In 1941 the Division of Research of the State Education Department released a report advocating the approach to the education of Native American students which Fadden had already attempted to implement. The report recommended:

> • Additional emphasis upon instruction in English—both written and spoken; appropriate subject matter dealing with Indian history, culture, and traditions for grades 6-8; and a syllabus of Indian arts and crafts for all grades should be prepared.

> • Arrangements should be made for the teaching of Indian history and arts and crafts by adult Indians on a part-time basis. (Birdseye, 1959)

Some educators of that time considered asking Fadden to introduce culturally relevant material to New York schools responsible for the education of Native American students, but Supervisor of Elementary Education Daly, then principal of the St. Regis Mohawk School, was instrumental in preventing this from happening. Instead Fadden found himself opposed by educational colleagues, members of the local white community, and political leaders. He was also denounced from the pulpit.

Fadden believed that formal schooling would not only be necessary for the continuation of Native cultures but could play an important part in the growth of these cultures. Prevented from incorporating Mohawk materials into the school curriculum, Fadden began the Akwesasne Mohawk Counselor Organization, whose members were primarily his students. Through education about Native American customs, traditions, and ways, members developed pride in their identity as Mohawk people. As a result of their many travels with the Counselor Organization throughout ancestral Haudenosaunee (Iroquois/Six Nations) territory, Mohawk young people met Native and non-Native people and had experiences which linked them with other Native Nations and the larger society. Also, as a result of their educational outreach as camp counselors and speakers to non-Native campers at summer camps throughout the Northeast, and to other groups of young people and adults, the Mohawk students became actively involved in countering the stereotypes of Indian people prevalent at the time. They were, essentially, cultural ambassadors.

Fadden's role in the Counselor Organization was essentially that of teacher and researcher. Under his guidance, the students sought out tribal elders in order to learn culturally relevant information, primarily Haudenosaunee oral tradition. Oral tradition (as opposed to written tradition) relies on face-to-face interaction and individual memory, and carries great potential for adaptation or embellishment. Although core elements of a story will remain largely constant, each teller may recount different versions of a story, depending on the context. The first time one hears a story, it is often a skeletal version which will then be fleshed out in subsequent tellings. The methods Fadden used at the St. Regis Mohawk School in the design of murals, pamphlets, and informational charts relied heavily on collaborative work between elders and students. The murals were painted over by a subsequent administration, but Julius Cook described the production in his introduction to the Six Nations Educational Cultural Historical Series. According to Cook, "The murals were worked out by the students under Mr. Fadden's guidance. They were in story form, each carefully detailed in accurate and authentic picture writing, colored and finished by various grades." The Counselor Organization members traveled as a group to Iroquois communities to visit with elders and take part in community events, essentially forming mini-research teams, learning by observation and instruction. For example, the counselors learned the significance of wampum belts by making facsimile belts. They learned to build various Native structures, mostly in miniature, and how to make clothes and headdresses.

These were all skills which were on the verge of dying out in Iroquois communities. Not only were Fadden's "cultural ambassadors" employed as summer camp counselors—their training made it possible for Native youth to draw on their own culture to become economically self-sufficient. Some young people became proficient in jewelry-making, others as multimedia artists and museum and film consultants.

As work progressed, Fadden taught his students to publish their findings, collecting and sharing information with each other. With Fadden's help, they put their findings and collections in narrative form, illustrating them when necessary. Some information was published in pamphlets, some in charts and drawings. These publications were then sold to produce revenue for the Counselor Organization. By 1948, the Six Nations Cultural Historical Series included twenty-six pamphlets and thirty-seven charts.

While Fadden was providing Iroquois young people with the means to retain and strengthen their Native identity and culture, he intended to reach an audience of non-Natives as well. Included within many of the pamphlet series was the following message:

> The future of our young Indian children depends upon the kind of history taught today. Our forefathers fought for their way of life. Our young warriors have died on battlefields all over the world in the interests of the American way of life. The American way of life originated in this country, and you may trace its birth in the history and culture of our ancestors, the American Indians.

The guide to the Six Nations Series contained a letter to the reader which stated:

> We have three reasons for publishing the Indian Material. One reason is that we want young non-Indian children to know the true history of our people. Another reason is that we wish to give our Indian youth a means of preserving their great history so that they will always have it. . . . Our last reason for the Indian pamphlets and charts is that we hope someday when we have all of our history down in this manner to raise funds from the sale of pamphlets and charts to erect a fitting monument to the great cultural leaders of our people, Deganwidah and Hyantwatha, the Founders of the Iroquois League, the first Peace League in the world. We feel that all nations of people, the entire world, should know of these great men and of the great work that they accomplished. People all over the globe could learn a lesson from these Iroquois leaders.

Fadden ended the Akwesasne Mohawk Counselor Organization during World War II, when he realized his students were being assigned high-risk activities in the armed services because of the skills they had learned. But by this time, the Akwesasne community itself recognized the value of this educational resource and considered the Fadden work their own teaching materials. People continued to read and treasure the old pamphlets despite persistent opposition from schools and churches. Gradually, however, many publications went out of print. Others were sporadically reissued; some survived in multiple generations of photocopies; and some were reprinted by agencies not connected with Akwesasne.

Although the publication of new pamphlets and charts ceased with the dissolution of the Counselor Organization, the work continued. Throughout his travels, Fadden had made many friends and been given many gifts, artifacts which then needed a permanent home. In 1954 he built a pine board structure on his land to house the collection which would become the Six Nations Indian Museum. The collection now includes a considerable array of artifacts dating from prehistoric eras through the American Revolution to contemporary times. One tragedy of much collection of Native American artifacts is that the objects were gathered without the stories which would reveal the context and significance of their use. At the Six Nations Indian Museum in Onchiota, New York, the stories are present.

The museum and the Faddens themselves have become influential resources, providing both information and encouragement to casual tourists, vacationing families, and Iroquois specialists pursuing interests in Iroquois culture. Some exhibits originated in the early days of the museum; some are new. Once seated on narrow wooden benches, surrounded by more exhibits than one could possibly absorb in a single afternoon, visitors are treated to "messages" delivered by a member of the Fadden family. These messages stress the contributions made by Native Americans to American culture and lifestyle, such as foods, medicines, and the American form of government. Questions and follow-up discussions are welcomed. The ever-present chipmunks, squirrels, and birds contribute to a setting which shows the Iroquois people as very different than the media has historically portrayed.

Sometimes, in brief moments, it seems that not only did the Fadden family choose to care for the artifacts which comprise the collection, but the artifacts chose the Fadden family to tell their stories and ensure the continuation of the Onkwehonwe, the Original People. It is an interactive, interdependent, and still evolving relationship. Ray Fadden, with the support of his wife Christine, founded the Akwesasne Mohawk Councilor Organization and the museum. Their son, John, and his wife, Elizabeth Eva Thompson of Akwesasne, continue the museum that Ray and Christine, began. John is an internationally recognized artist who has produced videos, drawings, and paintings reflective of Haudenosaunee culture. He is currently producing a new series of illustrations for the museum. Eva is widely recognized for her wildlife carvings, which include a series depicting Iroquois clans. She devotes considerable care to the collection and, with Christine, oversees the museum shop. John and Eva's two older sons, Don and Dave, have also been active in the museum, occasionally assisted by youngest son, Dan. Dave continues the storyteller tradition and speaks to groups about Haudenosaunee culture. An accomplished artist in his own right, he once belonged to a graphics group which used modern printing technology to feature Haudenosaunee artwork on T-shirts and sweatshirts. It is too soon to know the role of the fourth generation, but one suspects that they will be both benefactors and beneficiaries of the museum and collective Fadden family efforts which enrich us all by increasing our awareness and appreciation of Haudenosaunee and other Native American cultures.

The theory and teaching methods Ray Fadden was prevented from using in public schools of the 1930s and '40s seem revolutionary even today, in a time when greater emphasis is being placed on multicultural education. His use of diverse learning styles, his observation and subsequent application of Native instructional methods, his ability to actively involve his students in research and publication, his extensive use of field trips, and the establishment of a museum collection is unparalleled. The passage of more than fifty years has proven Fadden right: the people will continue.

Nadine N. Jennings

Memories

The memories which I love are these:
The fragrance of pine and balsam trees,
Coffee, herbs and sizzling bacon,
Sight of morning sun — newly wakened,
Fragrant ferns and new mown hay —
The smell of the woods on a rainy day,
Smoke of birch logs on a blaze,
A mountain peak above the haze,
The song of the whip-poor-will in the night.
The wavering fires of the northern lights,
The messenger bird's high pitched song;
The morning star above the dawn.
Crashes of thunder in the night,
The silver moon gleaming white,
The melody of an Indian song —
A shimmering lake in the early dawn,
Sweet odor of evening — these thoughts last
The spirit they cause, is never past.

These important Native American books
are available from your local bookstore.

Sacred Song of the
Hermit Thrush $5.95
(Also by Tehanetorens)

How Can One Sell The Air
$6.95

Basic Call To
Consciousness
$7.95

Native American
Crafts Directory
$9.95

Powwow
Calendar
$8.95

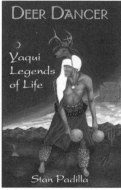

Deer
Dancer
$9.95